This Book
Belongs To:

....

Buster's
Story

story by Buster • written + illustrated by cheryl e. geller

This is the honest-to-goodness true story of a pants wearing, car riding, movie theater going, peanut loving, real life one-eyed rooster named Buster Keaton-Geller.

Buster was not always a pants wearing, car riding, movie theater going, peanut loving, one-eyed rooster.

In fact, Buster's story begins with Buster in quite opposite circumstances.

Buster's story begins on a very hot morning on a Caribbean island called St. John. Buster was badly injured and had collapsed from not having enough to eat or drink. He had collapsed in the middle of a road.

Buster was doomed.

Moments before he surely would have died, Buster was rescued and taken to Dr. Jan the vet. She prescribed water, food, medicine and love. Buster got all better except for his left eye. It was too injured to save, so Buster only has one eye.

Buster was too sick to live outside while he was convalescing. Since Buster slept on top of the computer during the day, he got a pair of his very own specially designed "fancy pants". That way Buster could poop in his fancy pants instead of on the computer keyboard.

Thanks to Buster's fancy pants, he lives indoors and he became a beloved pet. Turns out chickens have a lot of personality, are great "guard dogs" and love attention. They are easy to care for, are very loving and eat lots of healthy "people food".

Many foods that are safe for people to eat are not safe for animals to eat. Always make sure that any food you feed an animal is safe for that animal to eat. Buster eats organic grains, nuts, fresh greens, and some fruit but his all time favorite food is peanuts. Buster also likes red wine, but he is not allowed to have red wine.

To keep Buster from drinking red wine when you are not looking, put it in a glass that is too small for him to stick his head into.

Buster lives with twenty eight stray cats, two tortoises and a dog. For two months he even lived with an orphaned white-tail fawn named Blake. Even though Buster slept in bed with Blake, Buster did not like Blake. Buster was jealous of all the attention Blake got.

Buster lives with a lot of other animals, but Buster doesn't really like other animals. He likes people much more than he likes animals.

Buster has met other chickens. He likes lady chickens.

Buster's archenemy is Stinky G.
Stinky G. is a cat named Georgia
but her nickname is Stinky G.
because of her unfortunately
pungent and persistent halitosis.

Buster loathes Stinky G. because
she drinks all of his water on the
nightstand, she crawls on top of
him when he is trying to sleep
and she eats any peanuts he was
saving for later. Stinky G. doesn't
really like peanuts, she only eats
them so Buster can't have them.

Stinky G. is jealous of all the
attention Buster gets.

Buster has his own rubber ducky bathtub. He gets a bath about once a month, more often than that if he gets really dirty. Buster does not wear his pants when he gets a bath.

Buster always gets
a blow-dry after his bath
so he doesn't catch
a cold. Buster has
his own special
hair dryer.

Buster likes
his bath and
blow-dry.

It's like getting
tickled. Plus,
Buster loves
the attention.

Buster sleeps indoors in a hammock instead of a bed. Buster has to have water on the nightstand when he goes to bed in case he gets thirsty in the middle of the night. If he does get thirsty in the middle of the night and his water is is empty, he wakes everyone up with a *loud* "cock-a-doodle-doo".

There is a snowman lamp in Buster's bedroom.

Buster's never seen snow. That might explain why he often eyes the snowman lamp suspiciously.

Buster has a special bed
for his daytime naps.

At night the cats
take turns sleeping
in Buster's special bed.

But don't tell Buster that.

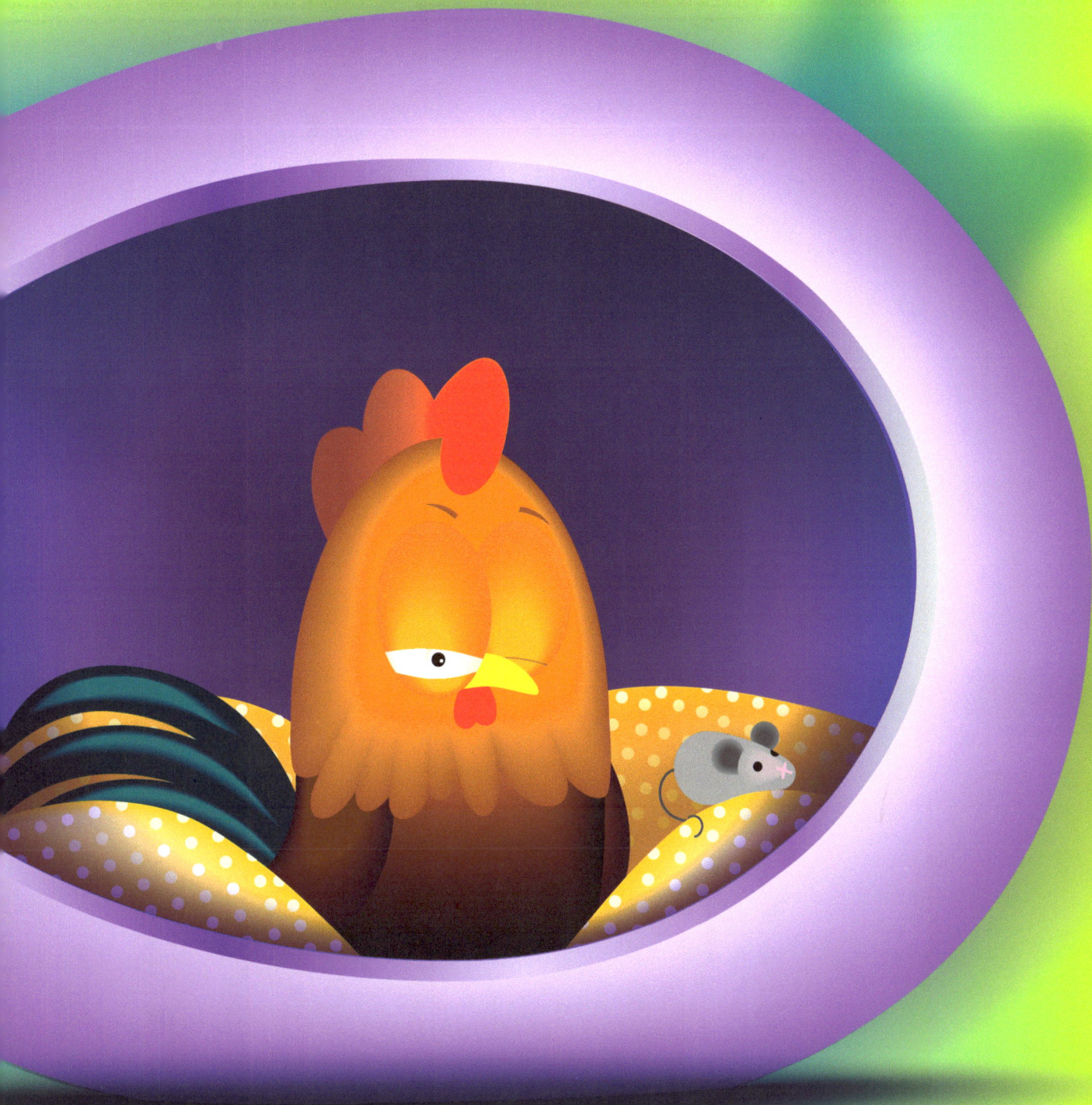

BKG's
Chickin'
Stylin'
Good!

A normal carrier
would not do for a
pet as special as Buster.

So Buster travels in style in a
vintage insulated vinyl tote.
Originally this tote was meant to
keep its contents hot. Now the
insulation helps keep Buster
feeling cool as well as
looking cool.

People usually laugh
when they realize there is a live
chicken in Buster's special carrier.

THE
BUSTERMOBILE

Buster has his own car.
It's called "The Bustermobile".
There is a special stack of pillows
for Buster to sit on so he can
see out the car window.

We call that
stack of pillows
"The Rooster Booster".

Buster enjoys going to the movies.
He sits and quietly watches the film.
He does not talk or cough.
He does not have a cell phone
that rings during the movie
and he never blocks anyone
sitting behind him. He is very
considerate except that he
hogs the popcorn.

Buster loves popcorn.

Buster is a rooster after all, so when he first started living indoors he would wake everyone up at dawn with a "cock-a-doodle-doo". That's why there are so many photos of Buster and the sunrise.

Nowadays Buster is used to living indoors and he no longer wakes up at dawn. He still gets his picture taken with the sunrise almost every morning, but now an alarm clock wakes him up.

Buster has fans all over the world who follow him on the internet. Buster gets recognized everywhere he goes and people throw parties in his honor.

So far Buster is taking all the attention in stride.

Oh he's a demanding and opinionated diva, but he was that way long before he became famous.

So, that's Buster's Story so far.
From certain death in the middle
of a road to becoming the
pants wearing, car riding,
movie theater going,
peanut loving, one-eyed
international online celebrity,
beloved indoor pet rooster
known as Buster Keaton-Geller.

Thank you so much for reading
Buster's Story. Buster hopes his
story shows you that just because
something is different or unexpected,
that does not mean it is wrong or bad.

Buster Keaton-Geller, St. John Rooster Extraordinaire

Buster's baby photo

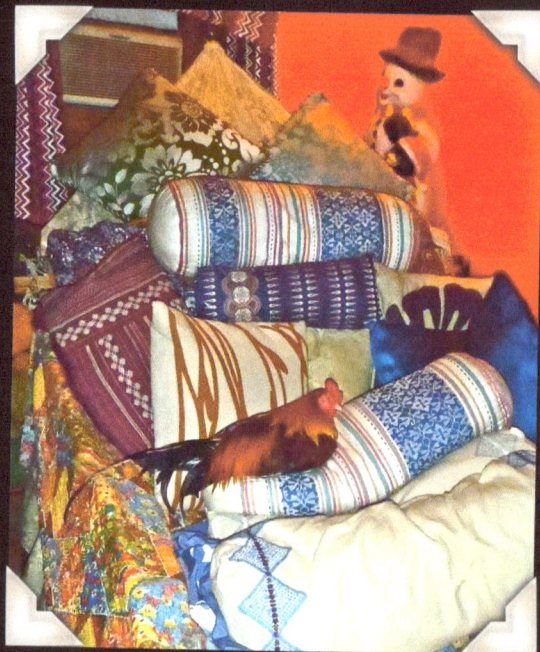

Buster in the hammock with the snowman lamp

Buster roosting on the computer

Buster in his bathtub

Buster and Georgia a.k.a. "Stinky G."

Supr fans Rus & Jeff taking photos with Buster

Buster in his "daytime nap" bed

Buster in his carrier

"The Bustermobile"

Buster & Blake

Text is 90pt Century Gothic Bold. Illustrations created on the island of St. John in the US Virgin Islands w/Adobe Illustrator.

www.ingramcontent.com/pod-product-compliance
Lightning Source LLC
Chambersburg PA
CBHW042023090426
42811CB00016B/1718